英武詠春

揚名四海

Austin Goh
Best Wishes.

The
Breaking Power
of
WING CHUN

Austin Goh

Published by Paul H. Crompton Ltd.,
102 Felsham Road, London, SW15 1DQ England
North America: Talman Company,
131 Spring Street, New York. N.Y. 10012, USA

Enlarged edition 1985

ISBN: 0-901764-647

Printed in Finland
Gummerus Printing, Jyväskylä 1996

The Author

Austin Goh, "The Author"
President of the Ying Woo Athletic Association.
Vice-Chairman of the European Lee Shing Wing Chun Athletic Association.
Master of the Wing Chun Academy in Ireland.
Chief Instructor of the Wu Shu Association.
Teachnical Adviser to the Irish Kung Fu Council.
Member of the Yip Man Wing Chun Athletic Association in Hong Kong.
Member of the British Kung Fu Council.
Member of the British Full Contact Association.
Member of the Malaysia Chinese Martial Art Association.
Member of the Martial Arts Commission.
Master of the Wing-Chun Academy in Switzerland & Germany

Training in Austin's Academy

Toughening Methods

Chi-Training

Training Using Weigh

Fighting Techniques

The Many Worlds of Austin Goh

Contents

Preface

Over the past sixteen years Martial Arts through the eyes of Austin Goh have been more than a way of life. He has been training since childhood in Western and Thai-Boxing together with his Chinese Martial Arts in Malaysia and Europe. A man of great ability and knowledge he always hoped that one day he would be qualified to promote Chinese Kung Fu to both the Eastern and Western World. He has now become the first Malaysian Chinese ever to have qualified to be an international Master in the art of Wing Chun systems in Europe.

He has used it as a stepping stone to launch many Tournaments. Demonstrations, Shows and also run several Martial Arts' Academies in Europe, United Kingdom, Ireland, Malaysia and even in Australia. He has also used the Art to heighten his success in a career as Bodyguard to the rich as well as helping in Night Clubs and Discos as a security officer. His affiliation with the Martial World has even involved him in doing Martial Arts Documentary Films for British Television.

A lifelong sportsman as well as a physical culture fanatic Austin has always been interested in training and trying out the latest Western and Eastern methods and equipments to improve his physique, power and speed into his training. He has now acquired weight training and roadworks training in order to condition the suppleness of the body and agility of the mind to add to his Traditional ways and systems. Austin always emphasises that whatever the Art one practises one must be practical and direct and Forms must be limited. All the techniques learnt must be put into use during sparring and free fighting in the Academy.

This type of training is important because it conditions one's reaction to any awkward situation that one might encounter in the street. Also a student must not waste too much time just perfecting a particular punch or kick to later find out that it doesn't suit him. Therefore a good Master should always try to show as many techniques as possible to find out what training methods are suitable for his students. After a number of years training and teaching in the Western Society. Austin realised through experience that we must learn the good from the past and cast away all the unnecessary training techniques which are more traditional than practical in our contemporary world, also we must learn the more scientific training and add on to our Eastern ways, then we can understand any problems that might obstruct our path.

We must be more open minded in our training systems and always want to improve and create better and practical techniques. There is no such notion that one particular art is superior, or even that a certain form is superior or even of a higher standard to another. This sort of thinking is irrelevant and old fashioned, it should be thrown out. A student should understand that all styles of Martial Arts are the same and are originally from the Shaolin Temple in China. The only and great difference is the person or individual who trains in the art and whether he has put enough effort and hard training in to develop the art he pursues, also he must seek the proper guidance from a proper and qualified Master. One must also understand that learning forms alone does not mean that a student can use it in practical ways, learning and training in school is very different to the situation one might encounter in the street. A practitioner who might have years of training in the Academy might even be easily knocked down by an experienced and tough street Fighter. Obviously understanding this a student will then realise that if Forms are not broken down into practical uses they will come to nothing. Forms training is beneficial to any individual to train for their fitness and health.

In 1974 Austin formed the Ying Woo Athletic Assosiation in the United Kingdom to promote Chinese Martial Arts especially the art of Wing Chun systems training. In the Academy a student begins his initial training with a series of intense physical training in order to prepare him to obtain better stamina and health to prepare him for the hard and tough training ahead.

From the Author

I have included here the latest training methods and both the Kicking and Pole Forms of the system which have never been revealed or taught to students unless they were a closed door student to the master, also different breaking techniques and chi demonstrations are fully illustrated in the book which I have carefully prepared over a number of years. I hope that after reading it the reader will develop a better understanding of the art of Wing Chun and hence widen the horizon for all the loyal enthusiasts in the World of Wing Chun.

Finally my greatest thanks for the help and encouragement I received from:— Master Lee Shing, President of the European Yip Man Wing Chun Association; Madeleine Goh, Secretary of the Ying Woo Athletic Association: Michael Lau. President of the Irish Kung Fu Council: my loyal students and Instructors in demonstrating the techniques shown in the book. Special thanks to photographers Peter Wilkie, Albert Cowan and Norma Harvey, without them this book might not have been completed.

My best wishes and luck to all in their pursuit of understanding the Martial World and to take care in their training . . .

Bil-Chee
Form

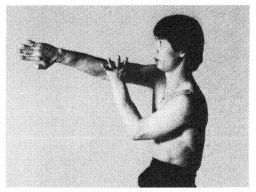

Kicking
Form

Pole-Form

Free-Fighting

Chium-Kiu Form

5

The Systems of Wing Chun

Training in the art of Wing Chun differs from school to school. Nevertheless all beginners start their training from the basic form of Sil Lim Tao. During this stage a practitioner will have to learn the correct stances, hands and breathing movements. Practising Sil Lim Tao requires undivided concentration and muscle relaxation. Exerting force means the forces are concentrated in the arms or the bridge of the beginner. After a year or two of training a practitioner will then understand the techniques and systems involved in the Form.

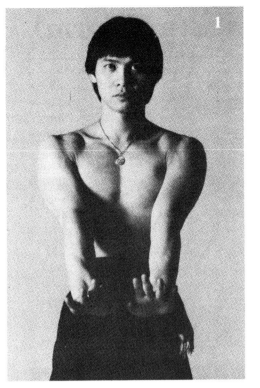

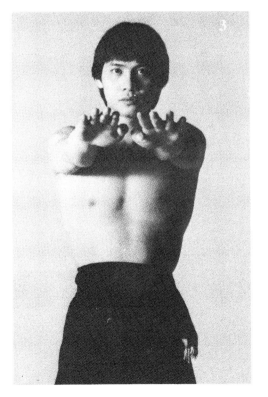

7

Chiam Kiu (Intermediate Form)

This intermediate form emphasises defensive techniques. Also during this stage a practitioner can train his footwork and the correct way to turn his body in response to his attacker. This form consists of different techniques and there are two simple kicks involved. The middle front push kick to the opponent's stomach and the low side kick to the shins.

The Traditional Wing Chun kicking systems are mostly direct and mostly strike just below an opponent's waist. After a student has mastered this form he will then have developed a good defence and attacking ability. From this stage onward a student should use the techniques learnt in practical ways like sparring and free fighting in the academy.

Bil Chee
(Finger Jabbing Form)

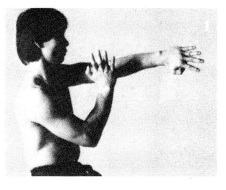

This is the last and most advanced form in the hand techniques of Wing Chun. It is taught only after a student has mastered or perfected the application of the first two forms. The outstretched fingers instead of closed fist are the weapon. This form requires years of reflex training and learning before one can become proficient, with constant training a student can attain an elastic flexible force instead of a rigid attack. This force in the Wing Chun system is similar to the force of the Crane and Snake movements in which the attacker remains poised to attack the prey and then strikes with a quick and sudden move. During this training the student is taught to attack the vital points of an opponent (the eyes, groin, throat, rib cage and nose). Therefore while practising the techniques of this form during free fighting, a student should be as watchful as an experienced Master in order not to create unnecessary injuries to his opponent.

This is the stage when a practitioner reaches his highest proficiency and free from all the restriction and rules in the art. Therefore he can be unpredictable and can easily surprise his opponent in attack as well as defence, in a fighting situation whether in school or in the street.

Therefore the art will become an art of self expression.

Bil-Chee *(Thrusting Fingers)*

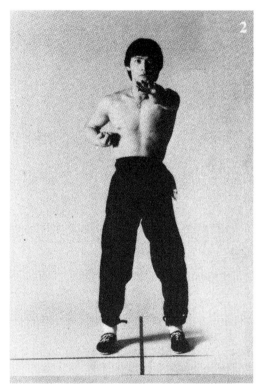

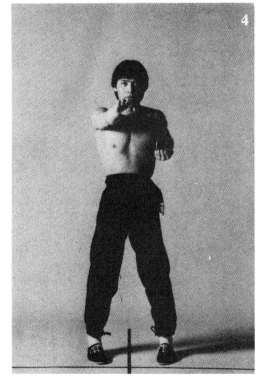

Double Sticky Hands *(Siong Chi Sau)*

This training requires great concentration and is practised with both hands clinging on one another while practising. It is similar to free fighting while one attacks without warning with both hands still clinging together; hence after much practise it will develop quicker reflexes, sensitivity and a better feeling on both hands of the practitioner.

Double sticky hands techniques are done in close contact and both the practitioners' arms or bridges should always be in contact during the training.

Once he is proficient in this training he will then move on to the next stage, the blindfolded chi sau training. Only now a student will find himself confident of putting whatever he has learnt to the test. With this training method he then has to rely on the messages received by his hands and arms to react to his attacker. I wish to remind the reader also, do not have the notion of thinking that a student can fight his attacker without even looking at him. This training system is to help a student to better his reflexes and the student's eyes should always follow movements and think ahead of him all the time in any situation.

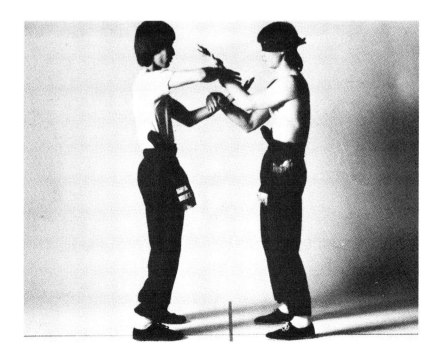

11

Training Sticky Hands with a Circular Cane

Constant training with the circular cane enables the practitioner to correct and perfect his hand techniques and position.

*Wing
Chun
Free
Fighting
Stances*

Close Contact Wing Chun Kicks

I find that a lot of people involved in the Martial World believe that in the Wing Chun systems kicking is neglected and is seldom used. This is basically judged from the three forms. The first form and even in the highest form, some footwork is seen only in the intermediate stage, a simple straight kick and side kick to the shin is seen. Also while practising most of the forms, the basic goat stance is normally narrow and practised stationary without even moving both legs. During sticky hands training kicks are seldom seen. I do not blame these people for having such an idea, in fact this is wrong.

There are, in fact, eight different basic attacking and defending kicking movements in the systems, and when counted on each foot separately we have sixteen different kicks, that is the left and right legs can both execute the same kicks.

All these kicks can be varied and changed in direction of attack or defence depending on the person who uses it.

The kicks are executed in a very short distance. It is direct and precise, therefore it is indefensible for most attackers. The practitioner can use both his hands and feet for attack and counter attack on any opponent in a very close situation, even less than six inches of space to move is sufficient for him. A very good example is that he can use his hands, elbows and feet to defeat his opponent in a telephone box.

Most of the kicking techniques appear to be simple and unspectacular, aimed mostly below an opponent's waist line. Nowadays the training is low kicks alone but high kicks are practised also. If a student has the chance of attacking his opponent's head to knock him down, he should not hesitate to use it. Why not grab such an opportunity? In my academy there is no restriction in training whether high or low kicks. A student is always encouraged to train more on the kicking techniques so as to build up a firm foundation. If a student is no good in his kicking ability he will obviously be at a disadvantage. A well trained practitioner can and should be able to execute his kicks to any part of his attacker whenever he wants.

I must emphasise that one must not restrict oneself in training in any form of Martial Arts. A man may be good in showing various forms yet when it comes to the realm of action if he does not know how to use what he has learnt all his training effort will come to nothing. As the saying goes. "Actions speak louder than words."

Kicking Form

Wing Chun Kicking Form

Front Push Kick

Bong-Sau Low side Kick

19

Low Palm (45°)

Turning Front Thrusting Kick

Quan Sau (45°) **_Push Kick to shin_**

Kang Sau (45°)

Fat-Sau side Kick

Lan-Sau (90°)

Low Push Kick (90°)

Slap-Kick

Bong-Sau & Knee

23

Bong-Sau, Low side Kick

Double Back fist

Lan-Sau (90°)

Front Thrusting Kick

Bong Sau (90°)

Bong-Sau (45°)

Turning Front Push Kick

Front Groin Kicks

28

Low Side Kick

Middle Side Kick

Back Fist & Sweep Kick

Front Push Kick

Slap Kick on Knee

31

Turning Lifting Kick

On Guard Position

Tan Sau

Front Punch

I would like to remind the reader not to think that by going through the Form in the book he can learn and master from it. The book is only a guide or reference to help a student to understand more about the training systems; the proper ways to train in the Form, like power, breathing methods, position, how and when to release the power, and the correct ways to turn and move the stance. All these are most important and have to be taught by a qualified Master.

Kicking Power Training

In training in kicking techniques a practitioner must also realise that he must have enough power behind him to knock his opponent down with the minimum of kicks or effort. The best and most practical Power Kicking training method is using the kicking bag regularly. After much training with the bag a student will condition his legs as well as improve the power in his kicks. Besides the bag training method a student should also use weights to help to improve the power in his legs, thus after much training with this system he can endure any punishment to his legs during his free sparring training. Power Training in the Wing Chun system is only achieved after years of hard training.

Power Training on Thigh Muscles
(all the energy for Kicking-Power is stored in the thights)

Improving Groin Kicks

Training for High Speed Kicks

Improving Thigh and Knee Joints

Hardening the shin bone with chopsticks. A practitioner must try not to overdo it by hitting the shin bone too hard at the beginning because it might do damage to it, as you all know that this is the weakest part on our legs.

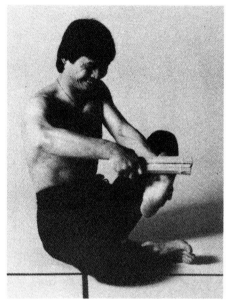

A top class Martial Arts Practitioner should know that he should be able to knock his attacker down with the least possible time and effort and he should also be able to absorb punishment from any punches or kicks that might be inflicted upon him.

Hardening the front soles with a bunch of chopsticks.

Kicking Technique Applications

Front Push Kick

The most representative of the kicking systems is the front push kick. To execute the kick a practitioner would firstly raise his knee and point the sole of the attacking foot toward his opponent's body and then later fully extend the foot to strike him with a quick and sudden thrust into his stomach area. The power is released by a quick reflex action from the thigh like a spring.

Side Kick

Side kicks are executed in close contact and are struck mainly on the side of the opponent's ribs and body.

Side Stamp Kick

This kick is to counter any opponent's attacking kick in order to stop his attack before he has the chance to strike.

Low Sweeping Kick

This kick is executed very quickly and at short range. Its main purpose is to unbalance an opponent's stance.

How to Counter Turning Spinning Kick

This is a very common kicking method used by a lot of Martial Art practitioners. It is quite a deadly move which aims at an opponent's head or body to knock him out. In fact it is not a difficult move to overcome.

Front Stamp Kick on Knee Cap

This kick aims at a vulnerable part of the opponent's body; that is the knee cap. If it is executed properly it can easily dislocate an opponent's leg.

Double Groin Kicks

This kick is aimed at the most vital part of the opponent (the groin).

The first lifting kick is a fake to attract the attacker's attention; once he tries to defend the initial attacking kick, strike at once with the other similar front groin kick.

Retreating Stance followed by Side Kick

This method enables a student to move back or retreat in case his opponent's charging force is much greater than his. He can avoid being knocked down by his greater force. To execute this move, simply withdraw the front stance or front leg and strike at once at opponent's body.

Turning Front Push Kick
to avoid direct attack from opponent

Lifting Kick

Lifting groin kick on opponent's thigh to stop front push kick followed by a low side kick on his shin.

Using Kicks against Two Attackers

Training Using Weights *(Physical Training)*

Weight Training plays an important role in strengthening our muscles and improving the power of a practitioner, in both punching and kicking ability. One must not be misled by those who use weights to build only muscle, the use of weight training in the Martial Arts is entirely different. The main objective of this training method being added to a student's course is to develop his speed and strengthen his internal muscles. The weights used are normally rather light, between 8 to 10 kilos and each exercise is repeated as many times as possible with speed.

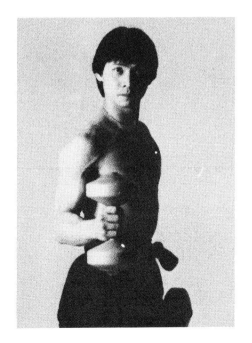 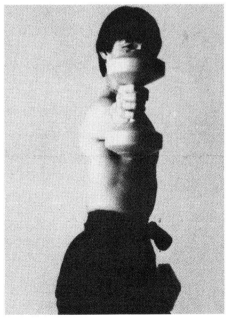

Turning Lifting Punch using Weights

Back Stance and Front Punch Training Systems

Back Lifting Punch — with Weights

Turning Back Lifting Punch for Power

Punching and kicking in the air enables a practitioner to loosen the tight muscles after all the weight training.

Inch Punch Training Methods

During this training a practitioner must concentrate on developing his knuckles, arms, shoulders, waist, knees and feet. After a period of solid training the power of all these parts will be concentrated into the knuckles.

Inch Punch Execution

Note: position of arm, shoulder and legs.

Improving the power in the Waist for better punching power.

Double Punching followed by Finger Jabbing Training to toughen the arm, wrist and fingers.

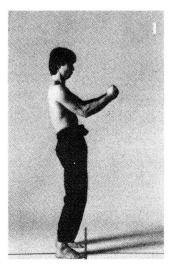  

Hardening the Knuckles by using a piece of light wood, a practitioner does not need to attempt to break it. This training is to let him get used to the breaking method.

Press Ups *(Endurance Training)*

Using the back of the hands. Improving the wrists and back thus increases one's power.

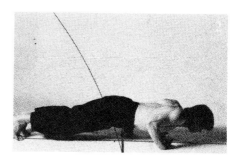

Using a lighter piece of wood for speed training.

One arm and finger press up if a student has achieved great improvement in the Inch Punching Training.

Using the pole to train the short distance power on the bridge or arm.

Toughening the Arms or the Bridge with cane or pole, enables a student to block attacking punches and kicks without hurting himself.

A bunch of Chopsticks is used too.

Wing Chun Pole Forms

Central Pole Technique For striking on opponent's throat

Ready Position

Lowering the pole downward to improve body stance and arms control

Square horse-stance Position.

Downward strikes.

66

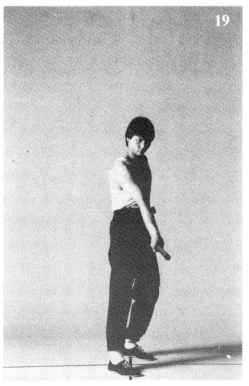

Finishing of the Pole Form

Chi and Breaking Demonstrations

(Photos of breaking, etc, by Norma Harvey)

Breaking with the forehead can be dangerous and needs years of solid training.

Breaking on the side of the head with a sledge hammer.

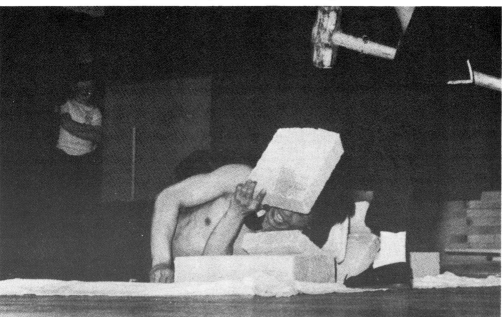

Using chopsticks as a weapon can be very practical and handy.

Using shopsticks as a weapon. This requires the use of chi as well as concentration and precision to release the chopsticks into a half-inch thick board.

Bending iron bar on the throat, a rare demonstration. To show the "chi" or inner strength of the Human body even the weakest part can be trained to the fullest.

A demonstration during the first Hong Kong Festival in Battersea Park, 1980. The stomach takes the full impact from a 14lb. sledge hammer, breaking five 4-inch concrete blocks.

After several years of intensive training a student can show his chi power by holding two chopsticks against his throat whilst Austin smashes them with a slap kick.

Full Contact Training should be practised with Protective Gear. The reader must also know that Competition training is completely different from Traditional Martial Arts training methods.

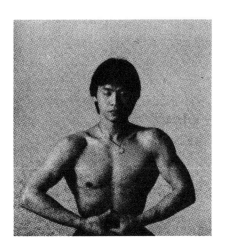

Meditation and Chi Training helps to improve a practitioner's endurance in his mind, patience and self control.

75

Traditional and non-traditional Martial Arts Techniques are also trained to the full.

76

History of The Wing-Chun Pole

Yim Wing-Chun was finally married to the man that she was in love with (Leung Bok Cho) who in turn taught the art to Wong Wah Bo who is a member of an opera troope on board a Junk which at that time was known as the Red Junk. The Red Junk was used as a secret meeting place for many Kung-Fu masters. There they made plans to overthrow the Manchus. In the travelling troupe there was an actor by the name of Leung Yee Tye who himself had learned a Pole Form from a cook who turned out to be Gee Sin, one of the famous five who fled from the Shaolin Temple when the Manchus burnt it down and was now hiding on board the Red Junk.

Both Wong Wah Bo and Leung Yee Tye were Kung-Fu fanatics. After a brief meeting they decided to exchange their skills and knowledge resulting in the Wing-Chun Pole which became part of the Wing-Chun System.

Altogether there are 6 1/2 strokes or strikes in the training system. The half stroke is incomplete in that the body is turned halfway together with the pole.

Basically the Wing-Chun Pole Form is simple and uncomplicated but it's fighting techniques are complex. There are thousands of ways of attacking and defending techniques with the poles and there is also the sticky-poles training system after the student has mastered the Form.

Sand-Bag Form *(Improve Breaking Power Training)*

The training on the sand-bag and kick-bag is considered to be one of the most important training systems in all Martial Arts. Punching and kicking on the bag enables a student to harden his knuckles and toughen the feet. He can also achieve the feeling of actually making contact with his opponent without all out sparring which, in the school, is considered to be unsafe and unwise. After years of training he can knock his attacker down with his hands and feet without hurting himself.

Training in the Wing-Chun sand-bag systems is different because most of the training techniques are executed in very close quarters to the bag. If one is trained properly a student can achieve close quarter or inch punch power for breaking or hurting his opponents within a few inches apart. Therefore it is important to practise the sand-bag form and techniques properly.

Sand-bag form is only taught to students who have already mastered both the 1st and 2nd forms (i.e. Sil Lim Tao, Chium-Kil) together with the double hands Chi Sou attacking and defending techniques.

Practising the sand-bag form is to prepare a student for the advanced form (Bil-Chee), some say that it is a stepping stone for the 3rd Wing-Chun form. The proper way to turn to avoid direct attack from an attacker is to train together with the correct ways and techniques and to use the sand-bag which is taught in this system.

I now reveal this form to the public for the first time as it is considered secret and is only taught to closed door students. I believe the times have changed and we also must change with the times and what was considered a secret in the past will not be a secret nowadays. In order for anything to survive it must be taught openly and properly, if not the arts will eventually disappear. If it benefits all Martial Art practitioners especially Wing-Chun students why not share it?

Breaking Power Training Systems

Breathing Control Training

In order to achieve maximum benefit of the breaking power and inch-punch power training a student must go through 3 different stages of hard training before he or she can achieve maximum power behind to break the object in front.

The first stage is to control the correct and proper ways of breathing before and after a punch of kick is thrown.

When a student starts training in the breathing systems, first and foremost he must try to stay as relaxed as possible and to avoid tension and stress that might occur in the body. Also it is preferable for one to train in the open, especially in parks, and make sure to wear loose clothing to ensure that nothing is in the way during the exercises. The best time for breathing training is in the early morning with lots of trees and grass around.

Once you think you have found a suitable place for your training: —

a) Relax your body from head to toe
b) Do light exercises to warm up the body (15 minutes)
c) Start off by taking in small breaths and feel the air or energy flowing into the lungs and all over the body
d) Breath in and try to hold your breath for about 10 secounds
e) When you exhale feel the energy inside your body trying to force its way out of your lungs.
f) Release the air slowly by controlling your lungs and repeat the breathing system 15 times, gradually increasing the number of seconds.

After you have trained and completely understood the basic breathing systems you can then move on to a higher level of breathing training. Do the same as before but this time feel the air or energy while inhaling flow to the right part of your body and try to relax the left part of the body at the same time. When you exhale try to feel the right part of your body actually forcing the air out. This is not easy at first but given time you will finally achieve it.

Physical Training

After training the internal systems (Ying) the student then moves on to condition the outer part of the body (Yang) physical training.

This training varies from school to school, nevertheless it is part of all Martial Arts training systems. It is more strenous and requires a student to repeat his particular exercises as many times as possible. I must stress that one must not over do it because it can cause more injuries than good if one tries to over train the body.

Physical training plays an important role in helping a student in training the breaking power of Wing-Chun.

Mind Control

The mind plays in important role in all training systems. It is important for a student to understand not only physical training but also how to train to calm the mind in order to co-ordinate it with the hands and feet in any situations.

Training the mind is similar to meditation training.

To start the training just sit on the floor facing the wall and with your feet crossed.

Then close your eyes and try to empty your mind of thoughts in order to clear you⌐ mind. Sit in this position for about 10 to 15 minutes.

Self Confidence
This will come naturally to a student if he has actually put enough effort into his training.

Method of Execution of Power
Anyone who practises Wing-Chun Kung-Fu must understand the proper ways and methods of executing the power during punching and kicking training.

Wing-Chun power is based on one principal, "Yau". "Yau" is that which is flexible so that if opposed by something stronger it will yield to the force and overcome its weakness. It is like a twig that bends with the wind but survives throughout the winter. Therefore it is hard to break a cane in two because it has the quality of "Yau". However a stiff stick will definitely crack under external force.

Before a Wing-Chun front punch is thrown the practitioner must relax his arm and shoulder and just clench his fist without putting a lot of pressure into it. He only releases his power and energy once the punch reaches the target (i.e. when the fist makes contact with the opponent's body). After he has executed his punch he then relaxes his arm and fist and withdraws the attacking hand to its original position, that is his defending position.

Wing-Chun men must always maintain the same magnitude of energy or force throughout because like a spring coil it must be flexible and springy.

Sand Bag Form (Sar-Pao Kuen).
1—4

On Guard Position.
5—8

Turning Front Punch

Low Lan Sau (45°)
(9—12)

Low Lan Sau
(13−16)

Turning Punch

Side Pak Sau Front Punch
(17 — 20)

Tan Sau Punch
(21 – 24)

Bong Sau

Quan Sau (25–28)

Quan Sau Advance

Double Punches (45°)

Quan Sau
(29—32)

Double Punch (45°)

Kang Sau

88

Kang Sau Front Punch (45°)
(33—36)

Tan Sau Front Punch (45°)

Front Pak Sau
(41–44)

On Guard Position

Bil-Chee (Finger Thrust)

Tan Sau

Weapons training is the highest form in all Martial Arts training systems. A top class Master should have the ability to perform and master both Knives and Swords as well as the Pole Forms and Techniques. Weapons training improves the movements, stances and co-ordination of the practitioner.

Final Remarks
People who claim to be the best in the Martial World are naive and do not understand the philosophy, mind and the real way of life in Kung Fu training that surrounds them. One should open one's eyes to search and look for more knowledge to improve and better oneself and should not stop learning in both the physical and mental aspects of the Martial Arts.

Even a Champion in the ring can lose out when confronted in the street where his attacker might surprise him with a weapon like a gun or knife. There is no fair play or rules outside the training school. A top class Martial Artist can even get knocked down if he is caught unawares. There is a Chinese Proverb, "Even a Tiger has to take a nap."

All Martial Arts practitioners whether beginners or Masters should always be modest and never boast about the skills they have learnt. They should never stop learning. The only time we stop learning is when we are dead and gone. People who learnt for only 3 to 5 years are considered beginners. Maybe after 15 to 20 years of hard training with the Master they might then have some knowledge in the Kung Fu World. Remember it is better to injure than to kill. But to avoid any form of combat in order to avoid any unnecessary injuries to one another is the spirit of a true Martial Artist.

It is also important for one to better oneself in all training and to win whatever challenge that might obstruct our path. Yet to win: "Friendship is Priceless."

Training in Master Austin's Academy — Ying Woo Athletic Association.

Ying means Courage; Woo means Martial Arts.

The Complete Wing-Chun Training Systems

Forms
1. Sil Lim Tao (Basic Form)
2. Arrow Punch Form
3. Chium Kiu (Intermediate Level Form)
4. Sand Bag Form.
5. Kicking Form
6. Breathing Form
7. Bil-Chee (Advanced Form)
8. Wooden Dummy 116 Movements
9. Wing-Chun Pole Form
10. Butterfly Knives Form (108 Movements)